Getting Th

Some people get there
by bike.

Some people get there by bus.

Some people get there by horse.

4

Some people get there
by camel.

5

Some people get there by car.

Some people get there
by helicopter.

Some people get there by train.

Some people get there
by boat.

Boat

Streetcars

All over the world, people get from place to place.

Balloon

Cab

11

Index